PRAISE FOR
THE SMART SELLING BOOK

"Truly understanding compelling reasons and compelling events
are critical to qualifying, forecasting and winning business.
Alignment to business drivers along with the appreciation of the
consequences of hitting or missing timelines (from those that matter)
are essential for those wanting a successful sales career"
Stuart Henderson, VP EMEA Field Operations,Symantec Inc

"In *The Smart Selling Book*, Mark Edwards hits the B2B selling
nail squarely on the head. His insights on modern selling challenges
will reassure you that you're not uniquely missing out. He doesn't
leave you hanging either, with practical ideas that will offer you
a way forward to improved sales results."
Garry Mansfield, Managing Director, Outside In Sales & Marketing

"Mark's writing style is incredibly engaging (his live workshops are just
as good!). We have all lost deals, large and small, this book helps to
highlight the reasoning behind these losses and equip us sales people
to ultimately win more than we lose – that's the game, right!? An eye-
opening read from someone right at the heart of our profession."
Ashley Brinsford, Global Account Leader, Symantec

"Mark Edwards' smart selling insights helped me achieve 400%+
target achievement and a six figure salary; sales is all about investing
your time in things that deliver success and reading this book is
one of the best investments you can make."
Blaine Craig, Business Development Manager, Diva Telecom.

"Regardless of how long you have been in sales *The Smart Selling Book* by Mark Edwards is very insightful and a must read. I will be issuing one to my whole sales team to digest."
Dan Merry, Business Development Director, Mobile Solutions Herts Ltd

"*The Smart Selling Book* humanizes and simplifies complex principles and engagements, breaking down every area and aspect of an engagement to allow us to consider how we can make changes for the benefit of all parties involved. I am an advocate of the checks and balances which Mark introduces into any engagement and I would urge everyone to pay particular attention to his thoughts around deal momentum, which I think shows real understanding. The fact that the book comes with fantastic sketches simply adds to the character and messaging contained within."
Ronnie Coupland, Senior Industry Executive for BAE Systems, Dassault Systemes

"Mark shines a bright light on the complex mechanics of winning that deal and breaks it down into simple, memorable lessons that can be applied to your next big project. Always engaging, clear and refreshingly concise, Mark takes the mystery out of how to close that sale."
Simon Waller, Vice President, Sales, GTT Communications

"Mark's latest book unravels the complex sales and buying process, helping sales professionals to quickly embrace smart selling techniques. This easy reading work breaks down the various sales strategies Mark has learned over 25 years into bite size chunks that will quickly help sales people become more successful. Anybody in sales who aspires to improve should read this book."
Adam Sheppard, President & CEO, Toshiba TEC European Retail Operations

"*The Smart Selling Book* simplifies the complexities of selling. In a complex world it is refreshing to be reminded of how few criteria determine whether a sale is a 'go' or a 'no go'. As the strapline states, use your brain and not your brawn."
Paul Fish, Director, Sales Enablement EMEA, Salesforce

Published by
LID Publishing Ltd
One Adam Street
London
WC2N 6LE
United Kingdom

31 West 34th Street, Suite 8004,
New York, NY 10001, US

info@lidpublishing.com
www.lidpublishing.com

A member of:

BPR
Business Publishers Roundtable

www.businesspublishersroundtable.com

© Mark Edwards, 2017
© LID Publishing Ltd, 2017

Printed in the Czech Republic by Finidr

ISBN: 978-1-911498-31-5

THE
SMART
SELLING
BOOK

USING BRAINS, NOT BRAWN, TO SUCCEED IN SALES

MARK EDWARDS

LONDON   NEW YORK   BOGOTA
MADRID   BARCELONA   BUENOS AIRES
MEXICO CITY   MONTERREY   SAN FRANCISCO
SHANGHAI

FOR OTHER TITLES IN THE SERIES...

CONCISE
ADVICE
LAB

SMALL
BOOKS:
BIG
IDEAS

CLEVER CONTENT, DYNAMIC IDEAS, PRACTICAL
SOLUTIONS AND ENGAGING VISUALS –
A CATALYST TO INSPIRE NEW WAYS OF THINKING
AND PROBLEM-SOLVING IN A COMPLEX WORLD

conciseadvicelab.com

This book is dedicated to all of those people who have bought from me – and also to those who did not. Although I earned more in the short term because of those people who bought, I probably learned more in the long run from those who did not. Go figure...

CONTENTS

Introduction

Many lessons in sales (and in life) can only really be understood with the benefit of hindsight – for with hindsight comes a broader and deeper perspective, along with a greater understanding of our strengths and weaknesses, and an acceptance for the vicissitudes in life in general, and in business in particular. Situations that produced seemingly successful results at one time may, at a later date, come to be seen as flawed – or possibly fortuitous. Conversely, situations that culminated in seeming disaster eventually can be viewed as turning points, powerful lessons or even stepping stones on an ultimate path to success.

It is also fair to say that luck plays an enormous part in the act of selling, even though the vast majority of salespeople fail to really appreciate this. Indeed, consider the chain of events that lead to a customer showing an interest in what you sell. Undoubtedly this interest has a major impact on the sales process – and yet the creation of this newly active need or interest may have had absolutely nothing to do with you. In fact, it might be due to another vendor's or competitor's failings. Lucky you! There are so many variables involved in making a successful sale, and so few of these are actually influenced or controlled by us, so it's quite amazing just how much reward and recognition a salesperson can get just by bringing in an order. As the proverb says, "success has many fathers. Failure is an orphan." For sure, many will seek credit for success in sales, and few will accept responsibility for failure – although in most instances 'the buck stops' with the salesperson. Perhaps in this instance we should say that, "Success has many fathers – but in sales, failure is an only child" (with the salesperson as the lone, responsible parent deemed guilty of the child's wrongdoings).

In sales, the difference between success and failure might come down to something as unmanageable as a comment made by a member of your customer's team during an internal decision-making meeting. Nothing you did or said. In fact, it was something that you knew nothing about. You win the deal and you're a hero, and you'll be having turkey for Christmas. But lose the deal and you are persona non grata heading for a performance management review and the loss of your best accounts.

With circumstances like these, you can perhaps see why selling is perceived as a precarious profession by outsiders.

With so many uncontrollable variables at play, we have to make the most of the limited number of opportunities we have for influencing and controlling the sales process. Having bought this book, it can be safely assumed that you are motivated to exert more influence and control over your own sales universe – and so it is with this in mind that we shall begin.

To help structure the contents, we will use the following diagram to map out the typical business-to-business sales landscape – with the sell-side/vendor organization on the right, and the buy-side/buyer organization on the left. Bridging the divide between these two parts, you will see both the sales and buying teams. The skill, expertise and approach of the sales team should be deployed to effectively work with the buying team and map out the **Complex Customer Environment**, aligning the customers' wants, needs and expectations with the offerings, systems and processes of the **Complex Sales Organization**.

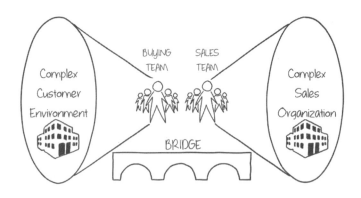

Diagram to illustrate the nature of the relationship between the sales and buying teams.

This model is intended to illustrate a conversation I once had with an IT consultant, who confidently stated that the collective experience of his IT department clearly indicated that the quality of service provided by a vendor was determined by the quality of their account manager and their sales team. In short, a great sales team (and a great salesperson) will leverage all the necessary systems, processes, people and partners from within the Complex Sales Organization to meet their clients' requirements, whereas a poor sales team or account manager will fail to do so. Same vendor, same offering, but with a very different result. It's worth noting that smart buyers in all fields are well aware of the critical role of the account manager, and so most are hyper-vigilant in their efforts to identify the true nature of the vendor's representatives. The whole sales process provides a smart buyer with an ideal opportunity to test the character and capability of those involved in the sale.

The insights and observations presented in this compact volume come from the work experiences (from the sell-side, buy-side and third-party advisor) that have been harvested over a quarter century of experience and thought. They are all very useful to me – and some of them may be known to you, while others may be new to you – invisible until now, even though they are highly applicable to your business. Don't take my word for anything you read: Test my theories against your own experiences. Consider them as you progress through the book by working through the various exercises presented. Only then will you see how the insights can be applied to your own world – and to your own advantage. Only then will you really be able to benefit from your investment in this book.

PART ONE

THE PERFECT
SALE

The Opportunity of a Lifetime.

To better appreciate the various concepts and strategies explored in this book, first I am going to present 'the perfect sale'. In this imaginary perfect sale, everything goes according to plan. There are no hitches, no complications, no delays, no problems – nothing that has to be addressed or overcome as part of the typical sales process itself. Every door opens. Every question is answered honestly and perfectly. Every feature of the product fits with a complementary requirement to the imaginary customer's situation. Once we have outlined the 'perfect sale', we can then explore areas where complications typically arise in a real-world, problematic and imperfect sale. My plan is to use the 'perfect sale' as a means of introducing elsewhere in the book the major trunk-road intersections, junctions, hazards, one-way systems, cut-throughs and detours that are commonly encountered in the real world.

Our 'perfect sale' takes place in a business-to-business (B2B) context (rather than in a business-to-consumer (B2C) context) in early 2017. I will simplify the 'perfect sale' simulation as much as possible, so that it's easily understandable – whether or not you sell products or services for large or small companies to global, international, national or local customers.

Ten years from now, it is likely that some of the complexities and complications of this case study will change, as has been the case over the last 10 or 20 years or so as our culture, common business practices embraced, and technologies employed have changed. I refer to this only for the reader picking up this book for the first time in 2027 (you'll know who you are...).

To begin, let me introduce both the sell-side and buy-side organizations and some key actors who will participate in our 'perfect sale' storyline.

Sell-side Background Information

John Taylor is a sales account manager for Fairland Video & Streaming Services Ltd (let us call them Fairland's, for short). John has been in sales for 10 years, and has worked at Fairland's for the past three. He is well respected and trusted by his co-workers and customers. John is very knowledgeable with regards to the various vendors, technologies and competitors that make up the video conferencing and streaming marketplace. He is also very well acquainted with how organizations use the various technologies to conduct business and the myriad benefits that can be gained by using video technology.

John Taylor

Fairland's is a reseller of video and streaming technologies and services. As such, it forms a part of a typical technology sales channel in which Fairland's buys products from a variety of manufacturers that it then sells to its own customers. Fairland's work with all the major manufacturers and vendors of high quality, enterprise-level video and streaming technologies – and due to Fairland's experience in this marketplace – Fairland's is recognized and well regarded by manufacturers, vendors, competitors and users.

John's workweek has him dividing his time between Fairland's European headquarters in London, working at home (in his video-equipped home office) and on-site at the offices of his customers and prospects. He works closely with a small number of sales and technical specialists at Fairland's and at the various manufacturers and vendors they partner with. Expert advice and support is always on hand, when required, by John for his customers and prospects.

Now let's look at the buy-side of our 'perfect deal'.

Buy-side Background Information

Hannah Ferraro is a technology expert who specializes in the planning, deployment and support of unified communications technologies. According to Wikipedia, unified communications (UC) is a buzzword for the integration of real-time enterprise communications services such as messaging, mobile and fixed telephony, video conferencing and other types of communication technologies. It is not a single product, but a set of products and services that work across different devices and different media types (text, audio, video). They are 'unified' in that they are all modern-day tools and methods for communications.

Hannah has a well deserved, high profile within the UC world and is often asked to speak on behalf of vendors at various conferences. In the last year, she has spoken at UC user conferences in Barcelona and Las Vegas to present her own perspective on the current and future states of communications technologies.

Hannah Ferraro

Hannah was recruited two months ago for the new role of vice president for communications at Coram & Capitan (C&C), an international law firm providing legal services for business and industry worldwide. C&C is already a well-established international law firm; however, in comparison to its competition, it has more recently been seen as heavily US-centric. This is where the vast majority of its personnel are located, and the firm has decided to expand its global presence and footprint by opening up new offices in Europe. Its new European, landmark headquarters is opening in London in six months, and new offices are also scheduled for Paris, Frankfurt, Madrid, Rome and Warsaw in the year ahead. This geographic expansion of operations and customer engagement is key to C&C's plans.

Let's start to explore some of the background of this opportunity.

The Coram & Capitan Opportunity

John is aware of Hannah's new role at C&C. They have worked together on projects in the past two years, when Hannah was senior director of communications projects at her previous employer, DexenData. John was one of the first people to congratulate her on LinkedIn when she announced her new role to her network of contacts.

The legal profession as a whole (and C&C in particular) has always been known to be relatively slow in adopting new technologies. However, now C&C sees how the latest videoconferencing and UC technologies can enable the legal profession to realize their desire to work with customers across a larger geographic footprint – while also helping lower costs and fees by reducing the travel costs associated with attending meetings in person. Part of C&C's future vision includes making the London office a central hub of world-class legal expertise, which can then be distributed effectively via video links securely and cost-effectively to offices in other countries, and their customers and partners worldwide. They see how video can help transform the legal profession for the better.

As an example, 20 years ago, an American partner might have flown first-class on Concorde to London or Paris to attend a meeting with a client (with all of the associated travel and accommodation costs and inconvenience). Whereas today, a partner can attend a similar client meeting, via video conferencing, without leaving the confines of their office. Time saved. Inconvenience avoided. Costs reduced. Everyone wins except the airline and the Four Seasons hotel chain.

Technical, Operational, Commercial and Decision-Making Considerations

Hannah has been put in charge of specifying and procuring the video technology to enable this vision. She has prepared and presented her initial budget request based on her existing knowledge of the market, and the budget request has been provisionally granted by the cash committee in charge of managing the expenses of opening the European offices. When her plans are finalized, she will need to make her budget request once again and make her recommendations to the cash committee to secure their full and final approval. Until then, the budget has been provisionally approved.

There are two technology vendors that Hannah and C&C will be considering: Techay Inc. and Tekbee Corp. The technologies are comparable high-end, enterprise-level technologies with each of their solutions carving out some small niche differentiators. C&C has equipment and services from both vendors in its offices across the US. In a rare example of true industry standards, the technologies offered by both companies operate well with one another – and as such, there is no technology lock-in that will make it difficult for a customer to use one or another (or even a variety) of their technologies in the future.

To add to the existing fair-weather conditions, Fairland's is also an award-winning 'Platinum Partner' with both Techay and Tekbee. It has nearly 20 years of experience in the marketplace, and it was a pioneer in the first phase of video conferencing back in the late 1980s and early 1990s (when individual room set-ups could cost $50,000).

Fairland's was also there through the development of newer, internet-based technologies in the early years of the 21st century – right up to today's super high quality, cost-effective solutions.

C&C's requirement for systems in London and Europe is known to both major technology vendors. Fairland's and four other video specialist resellers have been officially contacted by C&C and asked to respond to the written RFP (request for proposal).

Hannah's recommendation to the cash committee is ultimately going to be determined by a project team that includes herself; Matt Darcy, a London-based, tech-savvy corporate lawyer who has worked for C&C for 3 years, Phil Manly, an IT project manager based in the UK; and Seth Luther, an IT project manager and communications specialist based in New York. Phil works directly for Hannah, and Seth works for Hannah's US counterpart.

Matt Darcy   Phil Manly   Seth Luther

Timeline of Events and Milestones

To consider a simple sales timeline, let's work backwards and look at all events in relation to the eventual opening of the London office (which we will state as 'T', with all dates presented in terms of their proximity to 'T', as in 'T - 30 days' meaning '30 days before the T office launch day').

T
Office launch day

T - 7 days
Testing completed and systems handover to C&C
Testing takes place

T - 14 days
Systems installation complete
Installation and set-up takes place

T - 30 days
London site installation and set-up commences
Chosen supplier to provision and plan for project

T – 60 days
Supplier selection announced and contract awarded
Negotiations with shortlisted suppliers

T – 80 days
Supplier presentations and commencement of negotiations

T – 90 days
C&C to announce shortlist of three suppliers
Consideration of the proposals received by C&C

T – 100 days
Deadline for proposal submissions along with acceptance of C&Cs terms and conditions
Meetings and discussions to address requirement details

T – 130 days   Production and distribution of RFP and C&C
                     contract terms and conditions

Let's map some key milestones of Fairland's sales activity over this timeline.

In the weeks leading up to the production of the RFP, John and Hannah had a number of meetings, calls and emails to discuss, consider and refine the specific requirements for C&C. Aside from Fairland's, Hannah met with Techay and Tekbee to gain a better understanding of their future product plans.

John also met with Hannah's project team on a couple of occasions. Their meetings were professional, yet friendly and honest. John was made aware that C&C considered Fairland's and one other supplier to be the natural choice for the supply of this contract.

Following the meetings and discussions Fairland's recommended a blended solution with product from both Techay and Tekbee – with a 70%–30% split in terms of units and expenditure.

In our 'perfect sale' the customer agreed with Fairland's advice and so they were informed that they had won the deal.

Let's leave the 'perfect sale' here for the time being. We will come back and add more specifics as we continue to examine the deal in more detail.

Let's look at the various reasons why most deals don't look like this.

PART TWO

DEAL MOMENTUM: A CONSEQUENCE OF ATTENTION

Deals Demand Attention and Action.

There is a reason why the majority of sales opportunities die.

Most organizations that I work with typically expect to win only one in three, or one in four, of the deals their salespeople work on. Hence the statement made above, and condensed here into three words: Most deals die. That's an awful lot of time, money and effort lost for any business in general – and any salesperson in particular.

Of the deals that are effectively lost, they are lost in one of two ways. Some are won by a competitor, thereby condemning you to first, second or third loser status (depending on the number of active sellers in the mix); the others are lost as a consequence of a deal going cold with the customer making either 'no decision' or taking 'no action'. In these situations, you don't lose to competition, you lose to the customer's lack of will to pursue your proposal through to agreement. There may even have been periods during the sales process when the customer made such strong signs and declarations of intent that you thought the deal was effectively 'in the bag'. Or is it just me...?

To put things in perspective, that wonderful period of positive 'intention signalling' and 'peak interest' from your customer was a true indicator of their **intention** at that time – and their positive intention was a consequence of the actual **attention** they were giving and investing in you, your ideas and your proposal.

Reread that last paragraph and think about it some more before moving on.

To focus further on our point here: When your proposal got in front of them and had their undivided attention, they were hot for the deal: it made total sense to them; the numbers stacked up; and the value and potential benefit were crystal clear to them. But when their attention was diverted away from your proposal, their interest, enthusiasm and intent all waned. Without a compelling event (see chapter 5) to force a decision out of them, in time other priorities rose up and took their attention. Suddenly, they went cold on your great idea or proposal. The deal starts to slowly die without any customer attention. Other issues get their attention and focus. Sizeable periods of time passing with no actual progress only indicate that your deal isn't getting any attention – and unless you can get it back to the front and centre of the potential customer's mind, it may now be terminal. As Shane Kelly of HubSpot once knowingly declared: "Time kills deals".

Yes, you can still make attempts to regain their attention; however, the loss of momentum, interest and attention is not easy to rectify. Like a breaking news story that dominates the media's headlines for a while, it can't dominate for long before something else comes along, takes the spotlight, and the original breaking news story becomes old news. Boring. Stale.

Unfortunately, boring and stale is what can become of your deal too. The original idea or proposition that excited them and lit them up eventually became old hat. Old news. Just like you, they're human beings – and most human beings lap up novelty and variety. We have a natural in-built bias toward novelty and things that are new.

So what can we do to counter this type of situation?

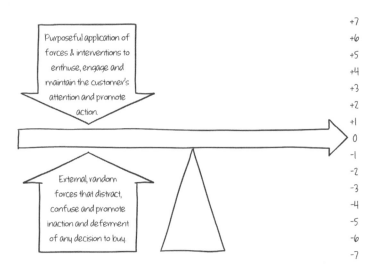

A diagram to help explain the opposing forces of positive and negative actions.

First, be aware that deals are 'hot' only for a period of time. Even the best-cooked food will go cold. The customer who is hot and enthusiastic about your proposal today may well not feel the same about it next week. And once things start to go cold, it will become increasingly difficult to get the customer to act and make any meaningful commitments.

As such, we must take appropriate measures to ensure that we can readily maintain their attention and enthusiasm for as long as needed for them to finalize an agreement.

You have to keep getting them to come back to the proposition with a fresh and enthusiastic mind. In a corporate setting this is not easy, as the customer has plenty of other things to focus on. However, you must do all that you can to keep your deal hot by keeping it in their minds, on their to-do lists, in their in-boxes, on their tongues during conversations, in their ears and in front of their eyes for as long as it takes to secure an agreement.

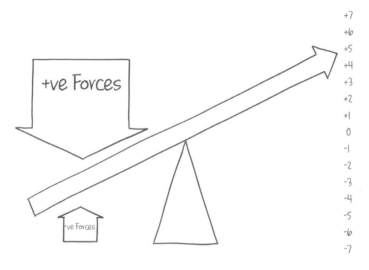

In this diagram we can see the effects of significant purposeful action.

Just checking in by phone or email to see if anything has progressed since the last call or email and hoping for good news reveals a lack of appreciation for the changing (and 'cooling') nature of a deal. 'Fiddling while Rome burns' is an expression that comes to mind to describe the watching and waiting that can start to kick in on many deals.

It is a mistake to expect a customer to maintain their enthusiasm and interest in your deal – over the time needed to get approval – without a future compelling event or an unbearable current situation to drive them, and without the creation of regular, ongoing, attention-focusing and interest-generating events designed to maintain or increase their commitment, curiosity and interest. Just because the deal has your attention doesn't mean customers will be thinking about it as often or in the same positive way as they originally did. This needs to be corrected. How often they think about your offer, and the way they think about your offer are two critical and highly variable factors that you need to attend to. Leave these to chance and you will find that a majority of your opportunities will come to nought.

Even if you are selling an incredibly desirable product (like a super-car for instance), the customer may cool off on the idea of upgrading if they get a fortnight to think about it after the amazing test drive that got them excited in the first place. In that interim period, things will happen: other competing demands, unexpected bills or expenses, or new, shiny trinkets and toys may appear on their radar.

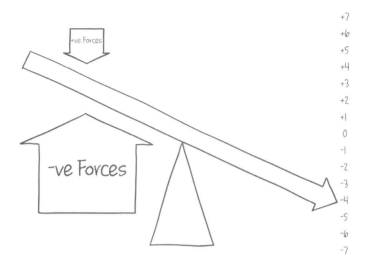

+7
+6
+5
+4
+3
+2
+1
0
-1
-2
-3
-4
-5
-6
-7

In this diagram we can see the effects of insignificant action
and how it is overpowered by negative forces.

Decisions are made in a moment – and that moment can be
easily lost.

That house you bought? You may have talked yourself out of it
if your attention and interest was taken away. That holiday? The
same goes. Heck, that purchase you made when you were on holiday (maybe some art or a watch or jewellery): without the sun on
your face and the breeze in your hair, you might have thought and
acted differently. All decisions are made in a moment, and they
depend on circumstances. They are based on emotion, and then
backed up with the necessary logic to support the decision. The
thinker thinks: the prover proves.

As for the sports car, if the test drive had been followed up with a 24-hour loan a few days later, along with a courtesy call the following day to see how the loan experience went – then it's likely that their enthusiasm for a new car would have been sustained long enough for the customer to allocate resources and make a decision.

In the corporate, B2B world, where the offer of giving a customer a thrilling test drive is the stuff of dreams, we have to work with appropriate events like scheduled meetings, site visits, conference calls, webinars, visits to other customers' offices, conferences, receiving demonstrations, whitepapers, lunch meetings, games of golf, trials or free use of products. All these demand some focused attention, and with the attention you can continue to make your case, to guide and maintain their enthusiasm and commitment until an agreement is secured.

EXERCISE: ANSWER THESE QUESTIONS -

1. What does your organization do to initially get your customers' attention and interest?

2. Score your 'attention getting' efforts on a scale of 1 to 10.

3. What does your organization do to maintain a potential customer's attention and interest until an agreement is made?

4. Score your 'attention maintaining' efforts on a scale of 1 to 10.

5. What could or should be better?

I am sure that your answers are quite revealing.

PART THREE

MUST THEY HAVE IT?

Is it a 'Nice to Have' or a 'Must Have'?

Something significant happened to the UK car market in the mid-1990s.

Gradually, and then all of a sudden, there was a change in the types of cars that were winding their way around the motorway network of the UK. Yes, the Ford Mondeo was still the biggest seller by far, with Vauxhall and Volkswagen still holding a large piece of the market – but there was a noticeable and increasing number of German cars making an appearance on the roads, and in the driveways of the cities, suburbs, towns and villages.

Mercedes Benzes, Audis and BMWs, once the preserve of company directors, were appearing in larger and larger numbers. This trend continues to this day, with the three German manufacturers increasing the numbers of cars they sell, and taking more and more market share from Ford, Vauxhall and VW.

As a reader of this book, it's clear that you have more than a passing interest in sales; in fact, I would hazard a guess that you are involved in professional sales in some way. As such, I would also hazard a guess that you drive one of the German marques listed above. Yes? No? Oh well...

So what happened in the mid-1990s to affect such a change?

Was it due to a change in sentiment towards German car manufacturers after the UK fully joined the European Union in 1992? We started to live, work and travel more on continental Europe, so maybe it was a sign of greater integration.

Was it because the Germans undercut the competition in a price war? No. That was not the case then, and it isn't the case today either. German prestige cars still command a hefty premium over the cars made by the more mainstream manufacturers.

Maybe their marketing and brand positioning gave them an edge? Yes, in this instance the prestige makers have always been very effective at making their products incredibly desirable. As Apple led the way in marketing their products as an integral part of a sophisticated and successful life, the prestige car makers also succeeded in making their cars a symbol of status and success. For sure, it plays a part in the reason for the up-tick in sales – but the gains they made were on the back of something else. Any guesses?

Let's start unpacking this puzzle...

	NICE TO HAVE	MUST HAVE
	Quadrant 1	Quadrant 2
CANNOT ACCESS PURCHASING POWER	NO WAY	HELP THEM FIND A WAY
	Quadrant 3	Quadrant 4
CAN ACCESS PURCHASING POWER	SHOW THEM AN EASY WAY	GO ALL THE WAY

In this matrix we show how your sales strategy must meet
the unique needs and circumstances of your customer.

The horizontal axis introduces the either/or concepts of 'nice to have' and 'must have'.

'Nice to have' is intended to describe something that is great to have, but is not deemed a necessity. Yes, it's relative: one person's 'nice to have' is another person's 'must have' – a walk down New Bond Street in London will prove the point (cashmere sweaters at £850!).

The vertical axis introduces another pair of either/or concepts. They are: 'cannot access purchasing power' and 'has access to purchasing power'. This is not relative. In terms of whatever the product or service is that you want, you either have access to purchasing power – or you do not.

Let us take a look at each of the quadrants, starting with Q1.

In this instance, your offering (product or service) is not absolutely necessary to the buyer. Maybe they don't really need it or maybe they already have something like it in place. They like it, but they don't need it. This means their motive to buy is below par, and when you combine this low motivation with a lack of access to purchasing power, you can see that this is an 'opportunity' that is going nowhere. In fact, it shouldn't really be called an 'opportunity' at all – because it isn't. However, there are plenty of so-called 'opportunities' entered in by sales teams the world over that would meet our criteria here: the customer sees the offering as a nice to have – and they don't have the budget or access to the person who has it. I will term this as being a 'no way' situation.

Moving horizontally to Q2, we have a distinct difference in the motive of the buyer. Here, the customer has to have your offering. Maybe they have a burning desire to own what you have to offer, or perhaps they need your offering so that they can complete some other action or project that they are responsible for. Their motive is strong; however, once again, they lack the necessary purchasing power. The difference in motive alone makes this a different prospect because in this situation the customer will move heaven and earth to find the funds. They might have to request the funds, or put forward a business case to get approval.

This is somewhat how children get what they want. To them, that new pair of trainers is a 'must have': a matter of life and death. But they don't have the money – so they go to the source (i.e. you) and start making their case. If their logic doesn't unlock your generosity, then they start to nag – until they get their way. I will term this as being a 'help them find a way' situation, rather than 'no way'.

Now let's traverse diagonally down on our matrix to Q3. Here we have a buyer who deems your offering as being a 'nice to have', and they have the purchasing power or the access necessary to buy. I call this situation 'show them an easy way'. The sale needs to be smooth and slick. Barriers and obstacles to ordering or fulfilment must be taken away. For the buyer, it needs to be made very simple and pleasurable if possible. To ensure a quick decision, an element of scarcity is effective at nudging the customer toward committing to the deal.

Last, let us move to the bottom right quadrant, Q4. Here we have the motivated buyer who sees your offering as a 'must have' and who also has the necessary access to purchasing power to buy. The best of all possible worlds. I call this situation 'go all the way' because that is what it is! If only all prospects were like this.

This model can be used to explain exactly what those German prestige car makers did back in the 90s.

With the introduction of a new type of finance agreement, and the inclusion of a significant 'balloon payment' at the end of the term, many people who would never have bought a German prestige marque were now able to do so. The German car was certainly a 'nice to have' to many people – but they were too expensive for most people's pockets. However, with this change in financing, a person could move from being a Q1 'no way' to a Q3 'show them an easy way' – and the Germans were very good at this.

Upon entering the beautiful showroom, the prospective buyer was ushered into the driving seat of an appropriate model. Ah, the new car smell, the look of the car, the solid feel of the bodywork. Very nice indeed. But, it's more than they could afford ... Surely.

Well, not quite, Mr Customer.

The new finance agreement, with its balloon payment, meant that the buyer was never going to have to pay for the whole car. In theory, they would just need to pay off the depreciation over the term, and the interest for the full purchase price. The 'show them an easy way' customer was now presented with a simple, easy plan that would mean they could be driving the car of their dreams in the next few days.

And that is how the German prestige marques made their move into the UK car marketplace.

Simple.

PART FOUR

THE DECISION-
MAKING UNIT

Understanding the Decision Making Process.

There are many occasions when an individual acts alone in making a decision.

At home, alone in front of the TV, you may decide to watch a movie, a football match, a game show, a repeat of an old sitcom, or any of the other myriad choices available to you. When joined by your partner, you may still hold the remote control, but your decision-making power may become somewhat diluted. Now, with another person's needs to consider, you may find yourself opting for a compromise. No longer do you feel free to make your choice solely upon your own needs; now you choose to take the needs of others into account.

This is similar in a sales situation. Indeed, 20 years ago, it was common for an individual to be in sole charge of making a buying decision. For a variety of reasons, the decision-making power within organizations has become more distributed. Decisions to buy, or to proceed with projects, have become subject to varying forms of consensus decision making. No longer do individuals seek to take responsibility and make decisions in isolation; the new norm is for decisions to be made by consensus.

In our 'perfect sale', Hannah is one part of a team tasked with specifying the requirement and determining which supplier (or suppliers) is best suited to deliver on C&C's needs. This group of people is commonly called the Decision-Making Unit (the DMU). In short, they are the group of people who will be responsible for making the decision. As to how they go about making their group decision, there are a few variations that seem to naturally occur depending on the status, dominance and psychological dynamics of the group.

In the rest of this chapter we will look at the features of a DMU.

Autocratic Decision-Making Units

You are probably well acquainted with the TV programme called 'The Apprentice'. The American version used to centre on the man who later went on to become the 45th President of the United States of America – President Donald Trump. The UK version centred on Lord Sugar (another successful businessman with an ego of a similar size as Trump's); however, his deliberations as to who should be 'fired' from the show each and every week were integrated with the perspectives, opinions and points-of-view of his two supporting judges (as of 2016 these included Claude Littner and Karen Brady).

This type of DMU should be seen for what it is: an 'autocratic' decision-making unit, where all deliberations will be guided by the central, dominant figure – and the ultimate decision (although being shaped and tempered by the two supporting characters) will be made in an autocratic way. Yes, there are a number of people involved in the DMU, but the final decision will be made by the dominant character. The secondary actors in this DMU are aware of their role, and accept it as part and parcel of being a part of the DMU itself.

Consensus Decision-Making Units

The second type of DMU should be seen as a more democratic unit. Indeed, this type of group sets itself up for a truly democratic decision-making process. In advance of making any decision, the measures by which the final decision will be made are mapped out and agreed upon by the group. Depending on the numbers of people involved, they may determine that the group needs to find a simple, numerical majority among the group, or in other situations, they may decide that there has to be a complete agreement among all members. It really depends on the types of people involved.

Consultative Decision-Making Units

Imagine (if you can) a DMU that truly blends the extremes of both authoritative and consensus-based DMUs. In this DMU, the roles and responsibilities of the members are determined and agreed to in advance, with all members feeding back their insights, concerns and questions to the group – with the ultimate decision being made by the person most qualified to make the decision. This is not necessarily the person with the greatest dominance within the group, but the one who is best suited to making a wise decision.

The Roles within the DMU

Within the DMU you will also find that people adopt specific roles and responsibilities. As in a football team, where players are allocated roles for goalkeeping, defending, managing mid-field and attacking. Here we will explore some of the more common roles and responsibilities: the decision maker, user, specifier, evaluator and approver (or ratifier).

The Decision Maker

This is the person who will ultimately be making the decision. In our 'perfect sale' example, this is the role taken by Hannah Ferraro. She is running the project and has been tasked with specifying and securing the provision of the required services.

She will ultimately make the decision, but this decision will also then need to be approved by the 'approver' or 'ratifier' (which in this case takes the form of the cash-committee – the people with the ultimate responsibility to approve or deny her recommendation).

The User

Remember Matt Darcy? He was described as the tech-savvy corporate lawyer in our description of the 'perfect sale'. Depending on his expertise, Matt's role bridges the responsibilities of 'user' (as he is someone who will ultimately be using the products day in and day out), specifier and evaluator. Indeed, his input may be required in all of these areas.

The Specifier

This is the person who will be responsible for specifying the details of the requirement. As an example, at a high level, a family may require a new car. However, the actual need is for a four-wheel drive, SUV type car, with seating for seven people and a dog.

In the 'perfect sale' the role of specifier is shared by the two technical specialists drafted in to the project: Phil Manly and Seth Luther.

The Evaluator

In some DMUs, the role of evaluator is separated out so that the person can act just as an evaluator. If a person acts as specifier, user and evaluator, it is likely that there will be some 'bleed' between the roles. The user with a strong preference for one feature, for instance, becomes a very weak evaluator on many other fronts.

In highly advanced procurement teams, independent evaluators will be employed. These are people with no technology, vendor or supplier preferences, but who will be guided by the specified requirement as it is set out before them.

The Approver

Ultimately, we all tend to go to another person for ratification and approval on any meaningful expenditure. The person with this role is often hidden from view, as it is a rare bird decision maker that will openly admit to the fact that their final decision is not actually the final decision.

The smart approver will typically 'approve' the deals brought before them – but will always reserve the right to veto a deal if they have a valid reason to.

The DMU Story So Far

Although our 'perfect sale' case study is hypothetical, let us take a quick review of the DMU once again and make some conclusions about its workings.

C&C's DMU is a Consultative Unit, with everyone involved in helping to specify the requirement and assess the proposals made from suppliers. However, when it comes to actually making the decision for C&C, it is being made by Hannah. Why? Simply because Hannah is the person best qualified to make the decision.

In the real world, you can find this out by actually asking the customer to outline the decision-making process they will employ, and to confirm who will be involved with making the decisions at each step of the way. Typically, you will find that the decisions are made collectively in the early and middle stages of the process (as in, which suppliers to engage with, what requirements are 'must haves' and which are 'nice to haves') – but eventually when it comes to making a conclusion, the decision will be made by one person, subject to taking soundings from the other DMU team members.

DMU Alignment

It is typically considered a self-evident truth, or tautology, when it is stated that: "People buy from people". The common-sense logic being that we are all people, and people prefer to buy things (even ideas) from people that they like; people they feel comfortable being with, people who are like them in some way. It probably goes back to our evolution and how it was a wise evolutionary survival strategy to only engage with and trust people who were 'like' you.

We should also consider the DMU team members with this in mind. Our measure with regard to the likability factor we will call alignment, as in 'how well aligned we are as individual people'. Are we closely aligned or at odds with one another?

This is a difficult and possibly impossible dynamic to engineer in many situations; however, it is one that absolutely has to be considered. If the 'chemistry' between buyers and sellers is 'off' – then it can and will impact their decision making. If there is no other logical alternative or supplier to turn to, then the bad chemistry can be ignored (just look at how politicians who despise one another can find themselves as allies in certain situations). However, if there is a viable alternative, and the alternative is being offered by a company, team or person with whom there is greater affinity and trust then the decision is always likely to favour them.

To determine the political landscape and personal alignment of the individuals involved on the purchasing side, we will need to establish some terms and their definitions. Some common terms used in this context include champion, supporter, passive and detractor.

At the very top of our list of wants would be to have the decision maker as a champion.

In the words of Mark Coates (a long-term customer, IT industry sales expert and champion of mine), a champion is a person with influence or authority 'who sells when you're not there'. Mark also uses the phrase; 'no champion: no deal'. And given the many obstacles that often have to be overcome or manoeuvred around in taking an opportunity through to a completed sale, then the 'no champion: no deal' maxim rings true. Indeed, your champion will promote you when you aren't there, take action to ensure momentum and real progress are being made, carry water for you, protect your interests, and promote you, your offering and your services to others. In fact, trying to sell without a champion can be considered a complete waste of time, especially when selling into a large bureaucratic organization that has many bulwarks in place to limit the actions of the enthusiastic and energetic. Indeed, in these scenarios, lacking an internal promoter to take action on your behalf, it's highly likely that your deal will stagnate and stall, leading to a long, slow death. Ring any bells?

In contrast, a supporter has a number of positive characteristics that are valuable to us: They like our product, they can see value, they even prefer it to the competition. However, they lack the commitment to our cause, the courage to confront any potential conflict and will back away from any situation where they feel that promoting us would involve any risk to them. 'Caution ahead' is their family motto. 'Rocking the boat' is not their style.

Still, in combination with a champion leading the DMU, any supporters can be a wonderful asset.

Moving down the scale of alignment, we have the passive. The passive is a truly neutral contributor to the DMU, with no relationship ties to any of the potential suppliers. This is a speciality of the procurement team. They are brought in purely to be objective and act as a brake to any rash, emotional decisions. They can be recognized by their less-than-luminous personality, their low energy, and lack of enthusiasm for you and your offering. Still, as long as they remain a passive in your champion-led DMU, then the balance is in your favour.

Lastly, we have the detractor: This is a person with a major concern or objection toward you or your proposal. There are numerous causes for the creation of this person: maybe your track record or reputation concerns them, or perhaps they feel unloved and ignored within the DMU, leading them to feeling resentful, or maybe they are more of an asset for one of your competitors for the account. Turning them toward your offering or isolating them within the DMU are your only options here. I would recommend a 'full-court press' effort to turn them into a supporter before even thinking about isolating them. Isolation should be your last resort.

The following table shows the varying combinations of 'Influence' and 'Alignment' for the various actors in our 'perfect sale'.

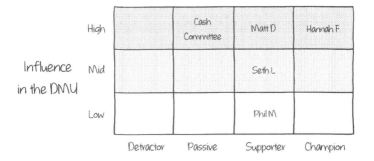

Alignment to you and your proposal

This type of matrix can be used to help you plan your approach and actions with the various DMU members.

EXERCISE

Use this type of table to review a number of your past deals. Map out the members of the buying teams on deals that you won, on deals that were lost to competitors – and on deals that ended up dying and now rest in the 'where are they now' bin.

PART FIVE

THE
COMPELLING
EVENT

The Force That Drives all Action.

After countless man-hours and hundreds of millions of dollars pumped into super-sexy customer-relationship management (CRM) platforms, it still seems that the likelihood of an 'opportunity' in the sales pipeline making its way to becoming a 'closed' deal is as bad as ever. In fact, it seems that it is getting progressively worse by the day.

Senior leadership now expects the pipeline total to be a minimum of three times target. Any less than that and someone will be having a 'hair-on-fire-pee-pee-dance' somewhere in the C-suite. Worse still, I have heard of companies where the ratio is x5, x6, x7 and even x9. The future looks bright … right? Nope…

Many strawman arguments have been put forward as to why the majority of opportunities in the pipeline never make it through to the end-zone. The emotional pain is real to all those who put in the effort, often banking their career prospects on converting opportunities to actual sales. The vast financial cost is there for the companies that expend effort and invest their limited resources in search of sales. As such, with so many people looking for an answer, there has been a steady stream of technology-based applications claiming their absence as being the reason why so many sales opportunities lead to nought.

The reality of why this situation occurs couldn't be further away from a technology solution. The cause is much simpler than that, and it also cannot be solved with IT.

What Does This Situation Reveal to us?

The numbers show us that most deals in the pipe don't close (you can also see it as 'pipeline on wheels', as I have heard it described before). Some of the opportunities are won by us and some are lost to the competition (maybe a quarter or a third in total) – but a mighty large slug of them suffer in a kind of endless, shoeless shuffle, just like we endure as part of an infinite queue waiting to clear an airport's passenger screening process.

The deals that aren't won or lost fall into two categories, where the customer decides:

1. Not to proceed with the proposed project (providing a clean break).
2. To put the idea on ice by postponing and pushing back making a decision – often stated as being for a short time, to be later postponed indefinitely.

The truth is that this type of customer decision indicates that they probably never stood a 'cat's chance' of making it past the finish line.

However, the more often this happens, the more often senior leadership will seek to find a solution, and the greater the coverage number that will be demanded of you in the future. And yet … it really doesn't have to be this way.

The emphasis of this book is to better understand and appreciate the complications and issues that stop a possible deal from making its way through the sales process and becoming an agreed-upon sale.

In our 'perfect sale', we are truly blessed by our customer having what is commonly known as a 'compelling event'. They have a date that they are effectively counting down to. Office launch day! This is a date by which everything needs to be in place and working – or else. The consequences of everything not being in place are just too painful to ignore.

In my opinion, the lack of a true compelling event is the main cause of deal stall, deal stagnation and deal abandonment.

Let me try to explain and illustrate the compelling event, and how it drives buying behaviour.

The best example I can think of is Christmas Day...

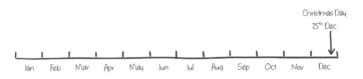

In this illustration we see the full twelve month run-up to Christmas Day.

On the 25th day of December, many people around the world will celebrate Christmas Day, and for many people the giving of presents is customary. Now, maybe it's just me, but I am not a lover of buying said presents. Why? Well, it takes time, it probably requires me to go to a major shopping centre, and when I don't know what to buy (as in, I haven't given it any thought) – well, the whole thing is just a nightmare.

However, I will buy – and I will buy before the 25th. Why? Because the 25th acts as the compelling event.

The compelling event: A date in time by which a decision or action must be made – or else – there will be consequences … often painful consequences.

It would be rational to buy some presents during the January sales (as some people do), but when do you buy your gifts? Are you like me, is it often last minute? See the activity peak in the illustration below. The one thing I know for sure is that I will **always** buy before the 25th. Ahhh. The power of the compelling event!

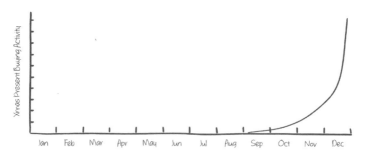

In this illustration we see how the level of activity increases most significantly just before Christmas Day itself.

It's Time to Start Qualifying Properly

Look at your pipeline. It is likely that lots of opportunities just don't have a solid compelling event. Sure, they might have a 'compelling reason' for the customer to buy – but the presence of a real, solid compelling event increases the likelihood of a deal being done to 100% (excepting major upheavals, unexpected events and natural disasters). Okay, so they may not buy from you – but the deal won't vaporize or end up with a 'no-decision' label applied to it.

There are many compelling reasons for you to start thinking about Christmas presents right now (get it done in time or make better buying decisions). But you won't – not until the compelling event date starts getting close. Until then, you may delay, procrastinate, or address other, more pressing or less difficult priorities.

Compelling reason opportunities don't need to be ignored or qualified out immediately. They do, however, need to be handled, cultivated and managed differently to secure a win, and this is something covered in the next chapter of this book. I also believe that these compelling-reason deals should be seen and understood by salespeople, sales managers and senior management as being materially different when in the pipeline.

Deals that have no more than a weak compelling reason are like wheelbarrows. When you're not there pushing the customer (and the deal) along, the deal just sits still. It has no momentum of its own, no energy from the customer, and you cannot force a deal like this across the line. You can, however, pick it up and move it toward the finish line alongside a willing, motivated customer.

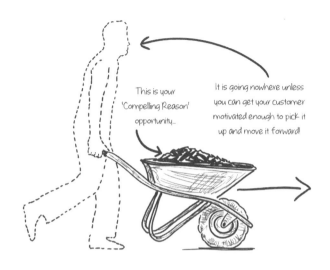

This illustration uses the analogy of a wheelbarrow to show the critical need for a compelling reason to properly motivate a customer.

However, an opportunity with a cast-iron compelling event is going to get timely attention heaped upon it, as well as lots of focus and resources from a customer. This opportunity is a zero-sum game; it will be won or lost. You win, or someone else does. No in-between. Unlike the inanimate wheelbarrow, this opportunity is like a London double-decker bus with your customer at the wheel – and the bus is travelling to **Dealsville**! You need to get on – and throw your competition under the wheels.

This illustration uses the analogy of a bus to highlight the great
benefits of having a compelling event (or a destination and
a scheduled time of arrival) in moving a sale forwards.

Start focusing on whether the 'opportunities' in the pipeline have
real, meaningful, cast-iron, customer-centric compelling events –
or not.

In our 'perfect sale', we have the compelling event of a new office opening, and all that entails. That new office opening date
is cast in stone. That date is stated in legal contracts. Insurance
coverage is set to start that day. Office equipment and furniture
will be bought, delivered and installed with that day in mind. The
day itself acts much like the countdown clock on a suitcase bomb
in an action movie. The closer we get to the time, the greater the
sense of urgency. Do you see how the compelling event works in
driving action?

So, specifically with your business in mind, what kind of compelling events are common? A contract end-date maybe? The start of a new financial year?

EXERCISE

Think back on deals won or lost in the past and reflect on the compelling events that drove the deals.

Also, think back on deals that ended up in our endless, shoeless shuffle purgatory. They were good ideas, maybe – but ideas that had no compelling event to force and drive action and decisions – and no committed champion to drive the deal into the end-zone.

PART SIX

THE
COMPELLING
REASON

The Long and Winding Road.

It is an unfortunate fact of life that many sales opportunities suffer the fate of being born into the world without a true compelling event. It is because of this deficiency that such sales opportunities will likely be dragged out, then delayed, postponed and eventually abandoned.

Yes, some sales opportunities without compelling events will live to see the light of day, but the majority of them will remain in the dark.

Do you remember that great idea you once had that remains unfulfilled and has come to nought? Maybe you pictured yourself converting your loft space into a cinema room, or you thought about starting your own small business, or learning a foreign language. All of them great ideas, for sure; just poorly executed with little or no application and effort.

With no deadline in play to defeat any indecision and force action, it becomes all too easy to procrastinate and put things off till tomorrow, or next week, or next month, or maybe next year, or the year after that – and so on.

You see, mankind is not in short supply of good ideas, or even great ideas. What we often lack is the ability to decide, commit, and then act until the idea is realized.

Sales opportunities that lack a compelling event to force and drive action just fall prey to the innate, energy-sapping traits of procrastination, avoidance and denial.

Now, before you seek to end it all and give up the most promising of careers, let us reframe the sentence that forms the second paragraph in this chapter so that it now reads: Although the majority of deals that have no compelling event will remain in the dark for all time, a substantial, highly valuable, albeit statistical minority of them will make it through to bathe in the sunlight. However, when there is no compelling event as such – there must be a compelling reason.

First, let's learn how to recognize this kind of opportunity.

It is possible that for too many (perhaps most) opportunities in your pipeline, there is not a true compelling event. In such a situation, the customer could or should act – but still they don't. Instead, they delay; they procrastinate; there is no momentum in the proposal; it drags; it gets pushed further and further down the road; they prioritize all sorts of other activities and decisions ahead of progressing your proposal. It's important to you – but clearly not to them.

These are the deals that move away from you. These are the deals that slip from one month to the next, from one quarter to the next. You know the ones, don't you? They are otherwise known as 'pipeline on wheels'.

This drawing illustrates the potential for a certain type of opportunity to continue to move away from closure. Deals on wheels.

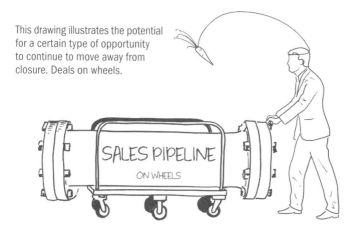

These deals have a very clear, rational reason for closing (e.g. they will save them money in the short, medium or long term, improve efficiency, add valuable functionality and increase sales). However, they all too often keep on slipping, with many of them eventually dying a slow and painful death through a combination of collective shame and embarrassment, and with an ever-increasing lack of enthusiasm and attention.

These are the deals that haunt you by the end of the quarter. These are the ones that make you look foolish for ever having believed they would come in. Maybe you have some like this right now ... right?

As you would imagine, our 'perfect sale' case study example comes with a compelling event that has a ribbon on top!

If the 'compelling event' is related to an event or specific date, then it follows that the 'compelling reason' is related to a sound 'reason' or 'reasons' for the customer making a decision. When there is a compelling reason, there will also be consequences for action or inaction. But the consequences are often not strong enough, meaningful enough, painful enough or beneficial enough to get them to act. Instead, they delay and defer: they give in to the gravitational pull of the status quo (aka, if it ain't broke, don't fix it) and they look the other way.

Let me explain what is meant by a compelling reason...

This illustration uses the analogy of a gas tank and
a pressure gauge to show the variability of motivation.

Let's have a simple, real-world example:

Every adult of a certain age should have in place a Last Will and
Testament to manage their estate and execute their final wishes
in the event of their death. This is especially true if the person has
dependents, as without a will there may be legal challenges relat-
ing to the future of the dependents and even to the distribution
of one's assets.

However, as compelling as this case is, there is a significant number of people who don't have one – even though they are aware of
the very real need to have one.

If there was a 'compelling event' for them on their time horizon, such as if they were about to have major surgery, then that would push them into doing something.

The logic behind taking the appropriate steps to putting a will in place is clear:

- It will ensure that your estate distribution and your wishes regarding your dependents are legally in place.
- Imagine! Peace of mind! Knowing that you have finally put a will in place. No more feelings of guilt followed by self-reassurance whenever the subject of wills comes up.
- If you do it now, then you have time to review the marketplace and consider the various options available to you.
- By getting organized now, you will avoid any last-minute panic leading you to act on speed rather than on actual need.

However, even with this list of compelling reasons to act, there is still a large group of people who choose to delay and defer the act.

Similarly, if you were to spend three hours online, reviewing and comparing your car and home insurance and other utility contracts, it is highly likely that you would be able to save yourself at least £300 a year.

Now, there's a compelling reason for you: Three hours and you can save £300 a year. Carried forward, that's nearly £1,000 in just three years with no ongoing effort required. Not bad for three hours.

However, it's likely that you won't do it, and will prioritize other activities ahead of it (a lie-in, a trip to the gym, some catch-up TV).

In these simple examples, you can see how a compelling reason is often not enough to get people to act. As such, we need to add some additional leverage to get the necessary purchase or traction to move things forward. So, let's look at some effective strategies you can use to counter the same willingness for customers to delay, to defer and to continue with the status quo within the business world.

Strategy 1: Do the math!

Make it a 'no-brainer' for them by doing the numbers and presenting the logic so that they can make a confident decision.

Too many proposals are only clear on one set of numbers – and that is the cost associated with buying the product or service. When it comes to calculating a clear definition of the return on investment, or value being offered (i.e. the efficiencies, gains, savings) too many proposals are very vague. They may make general promises to 'save money', 'increase efficiency' and 'reduce support costs' – but too often these 'claims' aren't backed up with any explicit calculations or sound arguments. The business case is flaky.

We often assume the customer can appreciate the potential value offered and promised – even though we haven't actually been explicit about it in our dealings with the customer. In fact, in many cases we have been downright obtuse (hat tip to Andy Dufresne) – hence, you and your proposal get sent to 'the hole' for a few months of solitary confinement.

In the future, get the customer data that you need to put the numbers down on paper and present the 'value' in a way that the customer can actually appreciate and understand.

If your proposal makes logical, numerical or monetary sense and can stand up to critical scrutiny, it is much more likely to get their focus and commitment. Make it a no-brainer.

If the customer won't give you the data or access that you need to 'do the math', then what does that tell you about the customer? It tells you that they aren't really that interested (or maybe they don't trust you enough yet). Be straight with them and tell them that you need the data to make the necessary calculations. If they won't play ball, then neither should you.

Strategy 2: Find, and then leverage, their primary driver.

If you aren't going to spend Saturday morning online comparing deals, then it's likely that 'saving money' is not a major driver for you. You probably make more than enough money already – or perhaps you are just financially irresponsible!

However, for a stereotypical salesperson, if I can connect the price comparison activity to a head-to-head challenge or perhaps a team competition, then all of a sudden the juices might start flowing – and three hours online trawling comparison sites now begins to look more like a game than a chore.

For the customer that isn't juiced by the savings, or by the improved functionality that your product offers, maybe the prospect of speaking at your upcoming user conference will incentivize them (for those who are ego driven), or maintaining a good relationship with you (for those who place a very high value on their relationships), or not wanting to be seen as a laggard by their peers (for those driven by what others might think of them).

Use conversations with people to identify the various drivers of the various people involved – and then link them to your proposition.

Strategy 3: Secure their public support, approval and commitment.

If I decide to go running tomorrow morning at 6am on my own, I may, depending on the weather, choose to either do as planned and go out to run – or go back to bed. However, if I commit to meet someone at 6am, I will be there come rain or shine. This human need to be seen as authentic and having integrity is widespread. Sure, there are a few flakes out there; but they don't tend to get into positions of authority anyway.

To leverage this human need, get your customers to publicly state their approval and enthusiasm in front of others. The more people they make this statement in front of – the more people involved – the more power it has. The closer those people are to them (in terms of relationship, status, contact and loyalty) – the more power it has. The fewer people involved (and in the worst case, maybe it's just you and them) – the less power it has. The weaker the relationship and the loyalty, the less power.

Ideally, you want to engineer situations where the members of the customer's DMU are publicly stating (in person and in emails) their preference and desire to proceed with the proposal. This doesn't guarantee that you won't be let down and disappointed, but it absolutely reduces the chance that it'll drag on. For many people 'my word is my bond' still means something.

In summary, to avoid living in a world of pain come the end of quarter, apply these tried-and-tested strategies. **Combine** these three approaches by working with the people in the client's DMU to strengthen their individual and collective drivers. **Gain access** to the data you need to **create a powerful, fact-based proposal and connect the gains to each person's drivers and agenda**. Organize face-to-face meetings, web-ex sessions or conference calls with multiple customer participants and **secure the public approval for your proposition.**

Finally, take a few minutes to review previous deals that you now see were eventually buried because the reason to act just wasn't compelling enough for the customer.

PART SEVEN

PATH
DEPENDENCY

A Journey of a Thousand Miles Begins With a Single Step.

At the core of a truly 'compelling reason' you will find a perfectly logical rationale. The logic to proceed with the proposed action will stand firm even though it may be subjected to various challenges and objections. The proposal to act, change, abandon the status quo and proceed with an alternative will just make sense.

However, not all situations are created equal. What might look like a 'no-brainer' decision from your perspective as a seller might not stack up the same way in the mind of a buyer.

Here are a few examples of what might look like exceptionally compelling reasons from a seller's perspective:

- "They will reduce their raw materials waste by 20% annually by using our technology!"
- "By adopting our approach to data storage, they will save money immediately on future hardware costs. The savings will run into millions in the next three years alone."
- "By outsourcing and using our service, they will save money and release themselves from the time and effort they put into doing it themselves – allowing them to focus on doing what they do best."

These are typical examples of the kind of argument that is put forward by enthusiastic sellers the world over. In each case, the seller's proposal makes sense. So why wouldn't the customer buy? Right?

What you will see here is how the seller isn't actually considering the full range of data necessary for the customer to make the decision to proceed with the proposal. Their claims to savings and efficiency are built on a limited view. Indeed, by ignoring any inconvenient information, the seller, only fools themselves. However, with a willing accomplice in the form of a suitably gullible manager, then perhaps the whole company can be duped into believing that the proposed deal really is on the verge of being handed to them.

Companies themselves are also commonly at fault here. Their marketing claims boast of performance and savings, but fail to take into account any of the more common, prevailing issues that would negatively affect performance and cost. It's just that real-world situations aren't quite as simple as that. Most decisions have to be made by taking past decisions into account. Those past decisions can often have an abnormally large effect on the decision being made today. This is what is called 'path dependency'.

A Wikipedia-type definition would state that path dependency explains how a set of decisions one faces at any given time are limited by, and dependent upon, the decisions made in the past. A personal example of mine is when I decided to move from Swansea to London in 1986. My decisions about where to live and work were from that point on affected by the initial decision to move to London in 1986. Moving to London and settling there effectively limited many future opportunities, regarding work for instance. Sure, the opportunity offered in Manchester is good – but is it a manageable commute? No. So, the first decision regarding where to live then impacted where I could work, where my kids would go to school, what opportunities would be available to them, and so on.

In our 'perfect sale' case study, we are faced with an ideal situation. A compelling event exists, and there are no financial, operational or technical ties to using a certain type of technology. In this sense, the opportunity can be likened to a greenfield building site where there is nothing to demolish, and no contaminated soil that needs to be treated or removed.

In technology terms, this greenfield site type of situation is quite rare. It occurs only in situations where the customer has no previous legacy decisions to consider. No previous financial agreements that would be difficult or expensive to get out of. No legal agreement that would be broken. No processes or systems that would be impacted by the change.

In fact, many companies have become extraordinarily effective at advancing their own causes by setting in play a series of 'lock-ins' that impact a customer's future ability to change, upgrade or switch to another technology, another vendor, or another way of doing things. These circumstances, often overlooked by sellers, are among the reasons why the logical decision is often to stay with the status quo, remain with an incumbent vendor or to stay put with the existing processes – even though change would ultimately be beneficial.

In these situations, the pain of change is just too great – and it is often the case that the incumbent supplier intended for it to be this way.

Change might mean financial penalties.

Change might mean ripping out and replacing lots of ancillary technologies.

Change might require that operations people have to learn a new system or way of doing things.

All these situations, and many others, make the pain of change too great to consider. And so, for these reasons, many companies continue to do things in a less-than-optimal way, using less-than-leading-edge technology and even wasting large amounts of cash.

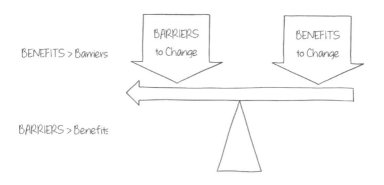

This diagram illustrates how the 'benefits to change' have to be greater than the 'barriers to change' in a proposal.

Consider the path dependency and lock-in strategies employed by two leading technology brands: Apple and BlackBerry. Yes, in this instance they are two tech companies and not a flavour for a sugared water drink.

Apple nearly died in the mid 1990s. Their approach to controlling their proprietary hardware and software in the late 1980s and early 1990s led them to become a small niche player. Their systems would not work with non-Apple products and the world was already dominated by PCs. In this instance, their lock-in strategy nearly killed them.

Most people see the rebirth of Apple as being all about Steve Jobs, great design and brilliant marketing. However, in 1997, just after his return to Apple, Steve Jobs brokered a deal with Bill Gates at Microsoft that threw a lifeline to Apple. In short, Microsoft would invest $150 million in Apple stock, and they would also invest and support the development of Microsoft Office for Mac. This meant that the vast majority of computer users who were path dependent on Microsoft Office products like Word and Excel could now make a case for using an Apple product. Then, all that Apple needed to do was to re-enter the market with the internet-ready, Office-enabled design legend, the iMac, and they could start to grow again.

However, although their rigid lock-in strategy nearly killed the company, you can still see how Apple pursues a walled-garden approach with their products even today. Apple products always seem to work seamlessly with other Apple products, services and offerings – and not so well with the products or services of other technology vendors. Once you have made the switch into Apple and become a Mac user who uses an iPhone, it becomes difficult to switch back. Yes, you can change, but there will be effort and costs involved. Mr Jobs has seen to that.

Let us compare this story to that of BlackBerry. Many of you will remember the glory days of the ubiquitous BlackBerry. A mobile phone with a qwerty keyboard and email. There was nothing to compare to it for years and so its sales grew and grew.

However, although it had many raving fans, eventually, when the user's mobile contract expired and the pressure to change to a smartphone became too strong, it was a very simple move. No hassle, really. Okay, no mechanical qwerty keyboard, but in its place, there was a great camera – and look at all of the apps available for it.

Cool apps didn't work well with BlackBerry, and so app developers started shunning BlackBerry, isolating it further, and it eventually went into a death spiral that it is still trying to get out of. Good luck with that.

Path dependency plays a central role in the story of these two companies. Indeed, path dependency plays a central role in the story of the 19th, 20th and 21st centuries.

Humanity made a decision many generations ago to industrialize using oil and coal. This decision determined the way our cities have developed, the technologies created and the way we travel. Now, even if there is a case for switching across to a greener, cleaner source of energy (say with an electric car), it is often illogical to do so because of the existing infrastructure; our habits and expectations have been shaped around an oil and coal economy. So, even though it is free to charge an electric car – do I really want to spend time charging the car when I am out and about? Will a range of 200 miles really be enough? In this instance, previous experiences and expectations around the ease of refuelling and the ubiquity of petrol stations will be enough to put most people off using an electric car.

I know two people with electric cars: one of them is a super-tech trendsetter so will overlook the downsides mentioned just to be one of a small number of Tesla owners on the road. The other lives in central London, has a Range Rover for weekend trips, and uses the electric car to get around town free of congestion charges, road tax and refuelling costs.

To revisit the seller benefits listed at the beginning of this chapter, yes, your proposal sounds great. By adopting your approach, they will save a lot of money going forward. However, to change technologies at this stage would mean scrapping an existing infrastructure that they have sunk large amounts of time, money and resources into.

As such, when weighing your compelling reason as to why a buyer should take your advice and proceed with the sale, be sure to take 'path dependency' into account. What financial, operational or technological decisions have already been made that now form the status quo and will effectively act as a bulwark against meaningful change?

Imagine how much more difficult the sale to Coram & Capitan would have been if the video systems for the London office had to run on a proprietary software platform that was only available from one vendor. Imagine that this system was not the best on the market. However C&C has been using it for the last five years, and if the new installation needs to work with the installed systems – then there are only two choices.

One is where you stick with the technology you have already got into bed with, in the full knowledge that it is not the best-in-class today, even though it was five years ago. Another is where you rip out and replace the entire video installed bases in all of your offices.

You may have the best technical solution on the marketplace, but in this type of situation, you can see how there is a more compelling reason for the customer to stick with the incumbent technology. The better alternative is just too costly to install world-wide and to do so will create massive disruption.

PART EIGHT

UNDERSTANDING VALUE

Reaching Across the Value Divide.

As is the case with beauty, value is in the eye of the beholder. You decide what you value. Society at large, our culture, the advertising that bombards your senses daily, and even your peers can try and influence you with regard to what you should and shouldn't value, but ultimately, it comes down to you. In the context of this book, we should agree that it comes down to the customer – the buyer.

Some of the things that we value can be objectively measured. For the most 'cost' conscious buyer, a £100 saving is absolutely measurable; whereas, for the buyer who values 'quality', this is a much more subjective value. One person's high-quality product is another person's low-quality product.

As such, to really connect with a person's needs, you must understand what a prospective customer really values. So how do you go about understanding what it is that they value? You ask them.

However, rather than just asking for a list of abstract values, it is worth spending time with the customer to get explicit details on how the customer defines, recognizes and measures value.

If we do this, then we can match our offering to their values, and in the fullness of time we can deliver on the said value. And by delivering that value, we can establish a significant, long-term working relationship, one based on understanding what is wanted and upon delivering that value.

Mapping out a clear definition of what a customer truly values takes time. But often, "you will find out at the end what you did not ask at the beginning" (hat tip to Abbas Meghjee for that belter of a line). Better to invest time at the front-end, learning about how the customer sees the world, rather than receiving a surprise Dear John letter at the end of the sales process informing you that your competitor offered a closer fit to what they wanted.

The objective measures that form a part of a customer's value map are easy to spot. They have metrics associated to them: pounds and pence, dollars and cents, megabytes, petabytes, kilobits per second, pounds, litres, ounces, miles, kilometers, square feet and prints per minute. All of these units are objective markers that make it easy to compare and contrast. They allow you and your customer to quickly assess that what you are offering matches their requirements.

However, when their stated value markers are offered up as generalized, conceptual terms, then pay attention, because these are exactly the kind of value markers that need to be defined.

For instance, a prospective customer might use phrases such as:

- We want a smoother workflow
- We want to eliminate the siloed approach to working that has developed here
- We want greater collaboration and communication
- We need greater agility in our IT systems
- We want greater efficiency and effectiveness

All of these phrases – and many more – are used every day in conversations between buyers and sellers. The buyer claims they want better collaboration and the seller claims to deliver greater collaboration. But what exactly do they mean by collaboration? 'Collaboration' is a category label you could use as a general term to include topics as diverse as 'working as part of a team' and 'being able to make use of a variety of mobile apps'. Which is it? All of them, one of them or none of them?

As such, we need to conduct a deeper analysis of what the customer means when they say that they are seeking greater collaboration. A soft exploration is called for; otherwise the exploration could begin to feel like an interrogation. Not what we are after!

The key here is to learn to spot the broad concepts, the generalized value markers when they appear in conversation and then explore them as they arise, or coming back to them at a later time. Seeking clarity on the terms being used by the customer indicates that you are doing your due diligence in identifying the customer's needs before making your proposal.

A simple, logical request for additional information is all that it takes. For example:

"We find that the term 'collaboration' is used by different companies and different industries in a variety of ways. As such, can I ask what are the specific areas of collaboration that you want to see an improvement in – and how will you be judging and measuring them? What are the priorities?"

Now, taking our 'perfect sale' into account with its DMU of four people, we must take into account the spectrum of values that may be held within the group: different roles, different wants and different needs.

As such, there is a matrix table that can be drawn up to show the various values within the group, and the value priorities of each individual. Then, depending on the power and influence of each person in the DMU, you can choose how to best construct your solution – and the way in which you will communicate your offering to the various members of the customer's DMU.

Your efforts to really get a handle on what your customer values will not go unrecognized by them, and your efforts will also help you create a snug, tight-fitting proposal that fits your customer like a glove.

Once you really know what they value and how much they value it, you can compose and present your proposal to them in terms that will ensure that you align your offering with their wants and needs – not only at the objective level, but in the more subjective areas too.

PART NINE

BUILDING A PLATFORM FOR FUTURE SUCCESS

Make Your Masterpiece.

To extend beyond the examples provided in our 'perfect sale', let's consider the development of the perfect account: an account in which there is a consistent flow of good volume, good margin business. An account in which you, your offerings, and your company are acknowledged as being the sole supplier (at best) or maybe the preferred supplier (at worst).

Your success in this area is critical to your long-term success. In fact, in my 30-year selling career, this is the one and only critical success factor that is common to all the top salespeople I have met. Let me come at it another way by saying that **the one common factor among all top salespeople is that they all have at least one big account.**

These top-gun type of salespeople differ in most other areas; their intelligence varies, so does their work rate, so does their approach to selling. I will state it again: **the one common factor among all top salespeople is that they all have at least one big account.**

In fact, some of the enormously successful ones have more than one great account. They might have two or three. Maybe more.

Your objective should be to do the same.

The mid-table salesperson will tend to manage a stable of mid-size accounts, and it is worth noting that small and mid-size accounts often require more time and effort than the biggest and best. Indeed, I have seen salespeople investing their time in accounts that can only ever serve up small, irregular sales opportunities. Eventually, this low return on time will prove catastrophic.

As for securing your big account, you may be lucky enough to receive a call from one tomorrow. You may already have an account that has all of the makings of one. You might have had one once, but you don't have one any more. You may be waiting to inherit one when the top guy in your team leaves or retires. There are many different sets of sales problems and circumstances – but there is only one solution to the big problem, and that is the big account (sorry, did I already say that the big account is important?).

An account like this has an ongoing need to buy. It is replacing old with new. Expanding. Moving into new markets. New territories. Acquiring companies. Bringing new businesses under their control. Investing in new technologies. The volume of purchases is far and away much larger than the typical account within your organization. This is where you want to be. A truly hegemonic, dominant, impregnable position within a strong and successful account.

So how do we get there?

Accounts like this rarely happen by luck or without a struggle. True account hegemony cannot be secured or maintained without rigor, thoughtfulness and consistent, strategic effort.

Imagine your hegemonic position within an account as a physical platform (just like the stage you will find in a theatre). Our hegemonic platform elevates us above the competition. It gives us a perspective that allows us to see opportunities and threats at a distance, and exploit, neutralize or address them in good time. It allows us to maintain our existing platform and extend it and raise it as far as the circumstances will allow.

In a true cultural hegemony (which is where the term is more commonly used) the hegemonic state dominates entirely the many areas that make up a culture and society. They dominate vital areas such as education, art, literature, science, politics, music, entertainment, publishing and media. Everything outside of their agreed-upon boundaries is excluded and drowned out.

If we take this example into the sales world, then to achieve true, big account hegemony you will need to build a platform that will help engineer complete dominion within your account.

Your platform is to be built using a number of solid planks, each plank representing an area of tactical or strategic importance within the account.

This illustration uses the analogy of how a strong platform is constructed from individual planks.

The various planks you will use to construct your platform will depend on the nature of your business. A pharmaceuticals company will need to plan and act differently to a financial services provider, as would be the case with a software vendor. Dealings with corporate structures and public sector bodies can also vary significantly.

A hegemonic account plan would include a consideration of the following areas:

Strategic Account Understanding

A broad, deep understanding of your account is a must.

- Who are they?
- What do they do?
- How did they get to this point?
- What is their business?
- Who do they serve?
- Who are their competitors and what potential threats lie ahead?
- What territories do they operate in?
- How do the territories differ?
- Where does the account locate its offices and its people?

Time invested in general reading about the company and their industry is time well spent in building out the breadth and depth of your knowledge. The knowledge can then be further developed and greater detail acquired via specific conversations both within and outside of the account.

The key here is to try to develop a clear big picture, which can also focus in on specific areas with a high degree of understanding. Cultivating a high level of curiosity and interest in your account can make this time-consuming process both enjoyable and rewarding.

Operational Account Understanding

Understanding your customer's business and appreciating exactly how they consume or use your services at an operational level is a major plank in building your hegemonic account plan.

I have often found that physical site tours are perfect for this. Getting to see the different units within a business and learning how they use your services will give you the opportunity to develop an appreciation that can prove incredibly valuable.

As an aside, it is also the case that hosting your customers to a tour of your business premises helps them better appreciate just how well your business operates. Drawing back the curtain on a business's operations is a sign of good intent, and will likely only bring both parties into a closer union.

Account Intelligence

Gathering useful account information and intelligence is also necessary to the creation and maintenance of your hegemony. Gossip, rumours, inside information, utterances or even assurances of impending changes and decisions from inside and outside the company have a function and a part to play in your ongoing account intelligence activities.

Each and every person within your company who interacts with the people within your client account is exposed to a variety of useful information as part of their dealings. Smart account teams leverage this exposure and create channels and means for everyone on the account to feed back information that is felt to be important or interesting in some way. The broader the range of sources, the bigger the net you have to collect information.

Relationship Mastery

An organizational chart is a great way to learn how an organization is structured in terms of authority and responsibility. From the top of the chart down, you can see the hierarchy of responsibility, e.g. this person has responsibility for these people, and these people have responsibility for these people and so on.

Understanding the responsibilities that have been granted to people is critical. However, in isolation, the organizational chart can give an incorrect picture of how things truly are within the organization. People are social creatures, not electrical circuits, and so relationships develop within the hierarchy. Some people are drawn toward each other, some are repelled, trust is established between some and undermined between others. In such an environment, a shadow organization develops and as such a shadow organizational chart can be overlaid upon the structural, hierarchical one. In this shadow organizational chart, we map out the powerbases within the organization. The factions. The in-groups and out-groups. Who exactly holds the power and authority – and who are the people who influence that power base?

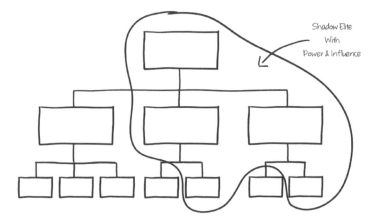

This diagram shows how to adapt a standard organization chart
to illustrate the hidden power and influence within it.

Beyond understanding the relationship dynamic within the account, your responsibility is to ensure that your team effectively
engage with and form as close a working relationship as possible
with the power players and other key influencers within the customer's organization.

Service Delivery and Customer Success

The best way to secure and keep a big account is to deliver out-
standing service. The opposite is also true, in that the easiest and
quickest way to lose a big account is to be perceived as unable or
unwilling to provide the service at the levels expected, promised
or agreed to.

There are many companies today that invest in 'customer success managers' to help ensure that the services bought are being delivered in accordance with the promises and expectations set out during the sales process. Also (and this is especially the case where new technologies, new processes or new behaviours are involved) the customer success managers aim to make sure that the customer's organization actually uses the service, and recognizes the value it delivers.

Most people have taken the plunge at some time and signed up for a membership at a local gym. Great facilities are available. Great spiel from the good-looking membership salesperson. Great intention for you – especially in the middle of January. However, fitting the new regime into the work-week isn't as easy as you thought it would be. Also, you picked up a bad cold in the second week and that meant you didn't go back until the middle of February. You tried a few classes, but you could never get into the one you really wanted so you ended up on a treadmill, sweating while watching TV. After taking a shower, you were getting home at 9pm and your evening was gone. The typical gym user will now begin to reduce their visits to the gym – although many will keep their membership running for about two years before realizing that it's not about to miraculously work.

Unfortunately, the business model for gymnasiums depends on this kind of attrition and non-attendance, and as long as there is another cohort of potential gym bunnies around the corner, then all will be well. For many people, the only practical solution (albeit an expensive one) is to have a personal trainer. In effect, this person works with you to help ensure you stick with the plan and reach the goals you said you wanted.

This is what today's customer success managers do – but in a business context. The aim is to make sure that when the time comes for an upgrade or a renewal, then the customer is well aware of the suitability, usability and effectiveness of your solution.

In a world where services are increasingly offered as part of a monthly subscription-service model, then customer success and satisfaction is the only thing (other than a watertight contract) that will stop them from switching away from your service.

Solution Superiority

To secure and maintain a big account, you have to be seen as being the best option among a group of potential suppliers. The 'best' is another one of those terms that can be used to judge a single measure (as in, which car is the fastest?). It is also used to signal a determination that is based on a potentially wide variety of measures (as in a conclusion based on fastest speed, most economical, comfort, lowest depreciation, service costs and manufacturer financial support).

Your aim should be to identify what your customer values, and to work at meeting and beating their expectations in each of these areas. Many years ago, I worked at what at the time was the UK's largest Value Added Reseller (VAR). In fact, I think they still are. One of their approaches to achieving and maintaining their position as the pre-eminent VAR in the UK was to conduct an annual customer survey. The survey comprised about 50 questions, giving customers the opportunity to rate the VAR's services, their people, the quality of their offering, the best and worst parts of their service, as well as providing an opportunity to define areas that they wanted to see offered in the future.

The results enabled the VAR to recalibrate their business every year and to address the priority areas as had been presented by the customer. This VAR is still number one in the UK. They have no unique product; they sell the same hardware and software as everyone else. Most of the companies they competed against back in the early 1990s have disappeared, while they remain. They have not moved from that top spot in more than 25 years. They are now so integrated into the UK IT industry and entangled in their customer's operations that it is unlikely they will lose their place at the top any time soon – or indeed any time in the future.

Path Dependency

Building your platform on great service is undoubtedly the best way to build and maintain your account hegemony. However, we don't live in a perfect world, and it is undoubtedly the case that your business rivals will be looking for ways to penetrate, land and expand within your account. Things will evolve and change within the account. People (even champions) may come and go. As such, you should employ a path-dependency strategy in the account, where any challenges to your hegemony can be thwarted.

This path dependency can be strengthened by layering dependency upon dependency, commitment upon commitment. Each one acts as a hook to secure your position within the account and to make your extraction difficult. The dependencies and commitments might relate to preferred or proprietary technologies, contractual terms and conditions, refunds and trade-ins, discount structures, operations and procedures in which you are embedded, relationship preferences, personal commitments, partner collaboration, shared resources and funded headcount.

The more embedded you are within your account's operations, and the greater your entanglement within their systems and processes, the harder it will be for you to be displaced.

Competitive Awareness

The legendary Chinese military strategist, Sun Tzu, said that the best wars were won without firing a single arrow. His meaning was that in the best situations, your opposition would just walk away, aware of their inability to inflict any meaningful damage upon you and secure any strategic advantage for themselves.

With this in mind, managing and maintaining your position when confronted by a competitor's well-funded campaign requires you to be always mindful of their presence and to the possible points of entry where you are most vulnerable.

'Know your enemy' is another well used military maxim, and it is one that you would do well to take heed of. An appreciation of your competitor's business, their offering, their people, the relationships they have, their strengths and weaknesses can only act to aid you in planning and decision making. To ignore their presence and their efforts would mean being either naive or wilfully negligent.

Partner Alignment

Referring back to the UK VAR, it should be noted that they resold the hardware and software of a large number of manufacturers. Their service and position were dependent upon the maintenance of mutually beneficial relationships with the various vendors they partnered with. Without the explicit agreement and support of those vendors, the VAR's competitors would have been able to breach their defences within these accounts.

In our 'perfect sale' example, Fairland's position as a supplier was supported by their partner status with the major vendors. Even though the major vendors will have partnerships in place with Fairland's competitors, their rules of engagement with partners will ultimately settle any possible conflict and disputes between competing suppliers.

Vendors will take a broad view when working with partners. The individual account will form just one part of their potential marketplace and a broader, maybe global account strategy. They have relationships to maintain with important suppliers. The vendor might back their bid in one account, but support their competitor in another account.

To ensure the support of your most valuable partners, maintain a tight working relationship with them and make sure that their support for you serves them well.

The world of partner relations can be a turbulent one, and at times looks more like diplomatic relationship between sovereign states, where past 'special relationships' are overturned as new relationships take their place. Ultimately it all comes down to self-interest in the end, and so decisions can often be predicted, as the logic of self-interest is so clearly apparent.

Strategic Planning

The major crossbeam in your platform, and the one that takes all others into account, is the role of strategic planning. This requires many inputs, much time and thought, imagination, vision, guile, pragmatism, wisdom, experience, patience and diligence. By ensuring that all the planks making up your platform are strong and secure, then your planning activity will surely be successful.

You will know where you are within the account – and you will understand where you can ultimately get to. Defining, scheduling and executing the various steps will eventually take over as you then begin to put your plans into action.

Use strong materials when building your platform. Set your structure right and put it upon firm foundations. In this way, your platform will see you through many years of success within your big account.

PART TEN

FINAL
THOUGHTS

Less Friction and More Value.

Nobody ever said a life in sales would be easy. Indeed, it is pre-
cisely because it can be tough that salespeople are paid as well
as they are. The trade-off between the difficulties and pressures of
the job and the increased rewards it offers is acceptable to only a
few – and you happen to be one of them.

The world of sales and selling is at a turning point. More and more
of the things companies and people buy are bought via some kind
of online sales engine or a virtual sales assistant. The majority of
today's first-world consumers are comfortable in buying online.
Very, very comfortable.

In fact, for many people, an impersonal online buying experience
is now their preference. Over time, they have grown to prefer the
way that online sales engines present the variety of offerings, the
alternatives available, and the way that any possible add-ons one
might wish to consider are offered. They like how an order's delivery can be tracked, and they value the sense of assurance this
gives them. Indeed, dealing with a person would, in many situations, now seem to be a terrible inconvenience – with no meaningful added value.

On the one hand, this shift towards buying via the internet must
be seen as a major threat to any number of sales roles. Why would
a company pay for the expense of a field sales team when their
customers prefer to deal with an online shopping assistant or a
corporate purchasing portal?

The threat to the professional salesperson used to come from other professional salespeople, whereas today, the threat is from some kind of online sales engine.

The growth and advances of online commerce are extraordinary. The way that revenues have been drawn away from traditional business and re-routed through a much smaller number of online providers is truly revolutionary. Google, Amazon and Facebook alone take a huge percentage of retail and advertising spending. It's not worth me quoting any numbers because by the time you read this they will be inaccurate: These companies are growing by 20% plus year on year.

If professional selling is to maintain a valuable position within our economy, then we too will need to evolve to make the buying process more fulfilling and beneficial for our customers. "Less friction" and "more value" would seem to be the keys – and this is where the interaction-rich world of professional selling can learn from the masters of online selling.

The masters of the online world have been able to make great use of the technological advances that have been made in the last 30 years or so: the advances in computing, the mass adoption of the internet, the huge advances in the connectivity speeds that enable fast uploads and downloads of files and videos, wifi availability, the ubiquity and utility of smartphones and tablets, the 'norming' of computing and the general acceptance of online alternatives for a huge variety of human, social, educational, cultural, economic and business needs.

However, to make this hyper-growth possible, they have also made masterful use of the discoveries that have been made over the last 30 years in psychology, social sciences and behavioural economics. Indeed, it is only through the application of various discoveries in these areas that the large-scale acceptance of online commerce, social media sharing, data collection, and the mass adoption of technology has come about.

Believe it or not, people used to be very cautious about conducting commercial transactions online and sharing information about themselves to faceless, never-before-heard-of corporations. Now those areas that once created friction, slowed down or stopped an online process, have become frictionless. In many instances, the friction is now reduced to just one click of the mouse.

Compare the ease with which you can buy a book on your tablet to how your in-house, clunky corporate systems operate. The former leverages the technology and psychology advances of the recent decades to create a frictionless, predictable process that you enjoy, whereas the latter is designed by some in-house techies who typically design systems to impress other techies – not users. Believe me, that's also how the internet used to be. I have been online since 1994, and it used to be incredibly painful right up until about 1999. It now just gets slicker, faster and easier by the year.

Now, if I read about a book in some article I am reading, I can open a tab in my browser and press "A" – the Amazon website address appears immediately (I don't even have to type it in anymore). I then type in the author's name or the book title, it comes up in the search, I click it, quickly compare the options available and decide if I want a hard copy or a Kindle version, select the choice, then click. Easy. So easy, in fact, that I buy quite a few books every week – even though I could never read them all. For me, the act of buying a book is so reasonably priced (when you compare it to the price of a quick coffee or a perishable sandwich) and the buying process so easy, that it has become one of life's simple pleasures. I'm taking an action and stating an intention to read it when I buy it – and there are no calories. It's a no-brainer.

Now to the future – and it is worth remembering the old quotation: "The future belongs to those who invent it." Think of the industrial revolution and how it was impacted by the inventive minds of Edison, Tesla, Ford and Marconi. They made life easier for people by eliminating much of life's drudgery. Remember also the beginnings of modern computer technology and the innovations of Watson, Wang, Gates and Jobs. Then the internet era and the second coming of Jobs, along with the new innovations from Bezos, Zuckerberg and others.

Some of these near-exponential gains in customer numbers, customer satisfaction and sales revenue growth are also available to field-based professional sales organizations. Most of today's sales organizations are already tooled up to their necks in tech: laptops, smartphones, wifi and 4G connectivity, CRM databases, browsers, apps, online content, enablement and marketing collateral. Technology firms have been very successful in selling the idea that technology is the source of the near-perfect gains and scalability that sales organizations and their stockholders demand. However, this "technological revolution" in the sales organization has not had a noticeable and beneficial effect for customers. In many instances, it is now more difficult for buyers and their sales counterparts to navigate their way through the various systems, processes and applications that have been implemented and integrated over the last ten years.

The next revolution in professional selling will not be technological, it will be psychological. The huge potential for gains in professional selling will be made by those organizations that work to understand and apply the advances that have been made in psychology, social science and behavioural economics. For it was the application of these same advances that facilitated the mass adoption of online communication and commerce. The online retailers and search engine providers could literally see where customers dropped out of a web session during their sales process. Rather than blame the customer and look for other prospects, they looked to themselves. They analysed the psychology that lay behind the drop out (too many choices, not enough information, no independent reviews) and then they created new versions of their website to negate any friction, fear, frustration or confusion. Step-by-step the psychology of the buyer was mapped out, the internet pioneers learned about how customers and users make their decisions, how they make choices, apply biases and heuristics (or rules of thumb) to understand their world, how they respond to changes, offers and suggestions, and how they could be guided into and through a sales process that was initiated by a customer who simply came to have a look and browse on their website.

This approach created platforms that make it easy and pleasurable for us to engage, because they are tailored to a set of broad psychological principles, as well as bespoke adaptations that are unique to each of us. The end result is a more pleasurable and friction-free experience.

For organizations that truly want to be perceived as being easy to do business with, they must also adapt the way their salespeople sell so that they also benefit from the advances made in psychology, social science and behavioural economics.

We can conduct sales in a way that better reflects our understanding of the psychology behind how people make decisions.

We can provide our customers with a well-organized set of choices and options to help them eliminate uncertainty and doubt as they consider the options available to them.

We can apply a series of psychological rewards to guide them through a sale efficiently, speeding things up for them and raising their satisfaction in the process.

The companies with the highest customer-satisfaction ratings are often the ones with the lowest number of interactions with people. As a counterpoint, it is worth noting that the companies with the very lowest ratings are the large, human-dependent bureaucracies where the person on the end of the telephone seems to have no idea what to do to resolve an issue.

In conclusion, the answers to today's sales problems are out there. They are hiding in plain sight. It's just that most sales organizations are looking in the wrong place. By understanding the advances made in psychology and behavioural economics and by then applying appropriate changes to the way that salespeople interact and work with a prospective customer, you can make a positive impact. You can reduce the inherent friction involved in many types of sales. You can increase your customer's satisfaction levels. You can deliver meaningful value as part of the sales process – and together, we can sell more and build a better business as a consequence.

ABOUT THE AUTHOR

Mark Edwards is an independent business consultant who delivers sales methodologies and advice to many of the world's leading brands and businesses. To date, his 30-year service record has seen him either selling, advising, training or consulting in a wide range of highly competitive industries and far flung geographies. He is the author of *THE VISUAL COMMUNICATIONS BOOK*, another of the titles to be found in the CONCISE ADVICE SERIES.